GUITARPRACTICE WARMUPROUTINES

Powerful Exercises & Technique Builders for The Advancing Guitarist

CHRISBROOKS

FUNDAMENTALCHANGES

Guitar Practice Warmup Routines

Powerful Exercises & Technique Builders for The Advancing Guitarist

ISBN: 978-1-78933-426-5

Published by **www.fundamental-changes.com**

Copyright © 2023 Christopher A. Brooks

Edited by Tim Pettingale

www.fundamental-changes.com

Over 12,000 fans on Facebook: FundamentalChangesInGuitar

Instagram: **FundamentalChanges**

For over 350 Free Guitar Lessons with Videos Check Out

www.fundamental-changes.com

Facebook: **ChrisBrooksGuitar**

Instagram: **Fundamental Changes**

Instagram: **chrisbrooksguitarist**

Cover Image Copyright: **Shutterstock**

Contents

Introduction

This book is the first in a three-volume series tackling the issue of practice. Two subsequent volumes will take the form of a 13-Week Guitar Technique Bootcamp (for intermediate, then advanced players), but before we get to that, I wanted to write a volume devoted solely to warmup routines and exercises.

This book calls upon more than ninety different drills, structured into ready-to-play routines that can be integrated into your current practice regimen, or used as part of the bootcamp practice plan I'll introduce for books 2 and 3.

Developing players will find this material to be a great source of mechanical and musical foundations to put them in good stead for further studies. Experienced players can jump into any routine and get game-ready for the day's work.

Each routine in the book is dedicated to an objective: prime the picking hand, stretch the fretting hand, run through scales methodically, or test yourself with some wacky finger and brain twisters.

Many of the drills ahead are ones I created for my own practice, and a few might resemble traditional exercises taught by guitar teachers for generations. In either case, there's a point to each drill, which I'll highlight as we go.

You can select a routine according to your goals and work through it or create your own *à la carte* regimen from various chapters. To do so, try each routine, then note the drills suited to your level and related to your goals. There's enough material to ensure you can create many versions of the ideal warmup routine.

My most important advice about warming up is that *your warmup should not be more difficult than your workload.*

Often, I see exercises presented as warmups that begin with strenuous stretches and intricate picking patterns. While testing and pushing technique to its limits is important, I don't believe that doing so is the best way to begin.

Ease in – there's plenty of time to loosen up! We'll get to the crazy stretches and unusual atonal sequences later in the book.

With up to ten exercises in each routine, you'll likely have time to play each exercise a few times or even combine a couple of routines to prep your hands for the day's principal work. Once you've completed your warmup, you can begin your official practice routine.

Since your main objective is to get the blood flowing and the hands limber, I don't prescribe heavy metronome usage for these exercises. Save that for tempo training and speed development.

For now, find a pace suited to how tight or loose your muscles feel, and always listen to your body. At the first sign of pain or strain, shake off any tension and proceed cautiously.

To spare you an excess of mechanical jargon in the descriptions, I've performed each routine on video so you can see the specifics of my technique up close.

I hope you enjoy these routines. I've had fun putting these drills together and distilling years of practice into them.

Chris Brooks

Get the Audio

The audio files for this book are available to download for free from **www.fundamental-changes.com**. The link is in the top right-hand corner. Click "Download Audio" and choose your instrument. Select the title of this book from the menu, and complete the form to get your audio.

We recommend that you download the files directly to your computer (not to your tablet or phone) and extract them there before adding them to your media library. If you encounter any difficulty, we provide technical support within 24 hours via the contact form.

Get the Video:

See how every routine in the book should be played with this bonus video content! Visit:

https://fundamental-changes.teachable.com/p/warmups

Or scan the QR code below with your smartphone:

For over 350 free guitar lessons with videos check out:

www.fundamental-changes.com

Join our free Facebook Community of Cool Musicians

www.facebook.com/groups/fundamentalguitar

Tag us for a share on Instagram: **FundamentalChanges**

The Pre-Warmup

Before practice, it's a good idea to stand up, have a stretch, do some shoulder rolls, and shake your wrists a few times.

I also like to perform some basic massage on my wrists, forearms, and chest to release any tension.

This is my personal pre-warmup, which is not intended to replace expert medical or therapeutic advice for any injuries you may be experiencing. Please consult a professional if you have ongoing issues with muscle tension or injury. Disclaimer complete!

I begin my self-massage on the inside of both of my forearms, using the thumb of the opposite hand to move from side to side with just enough pressure to loosen up.

To relax the wrists, I use my thumbs to make circular motions, clockwise and anticlockwise for each hand. I perform these circles from various points if I notice any tightness.

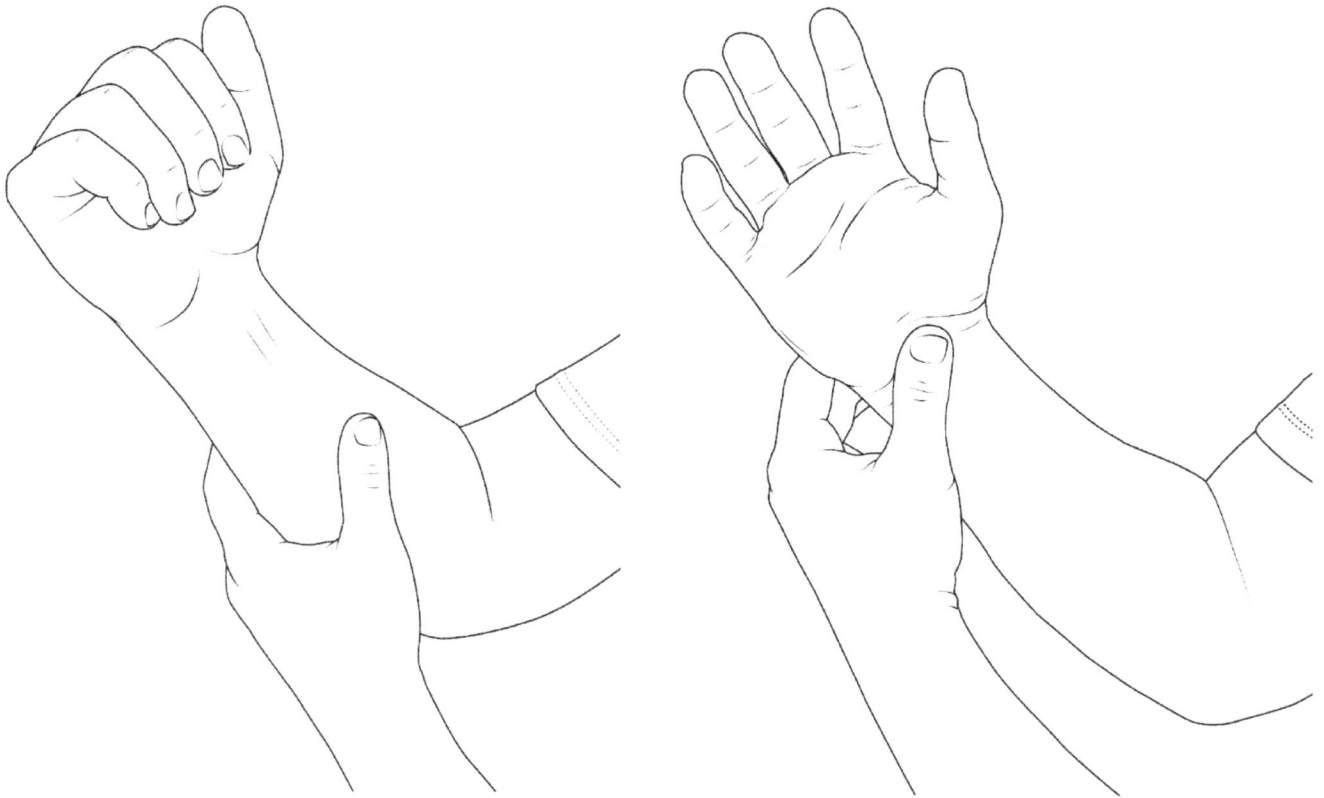

On the outside of the forearm, I perform another sideways motion with my thumb. This helps my picking-hand side in particular.

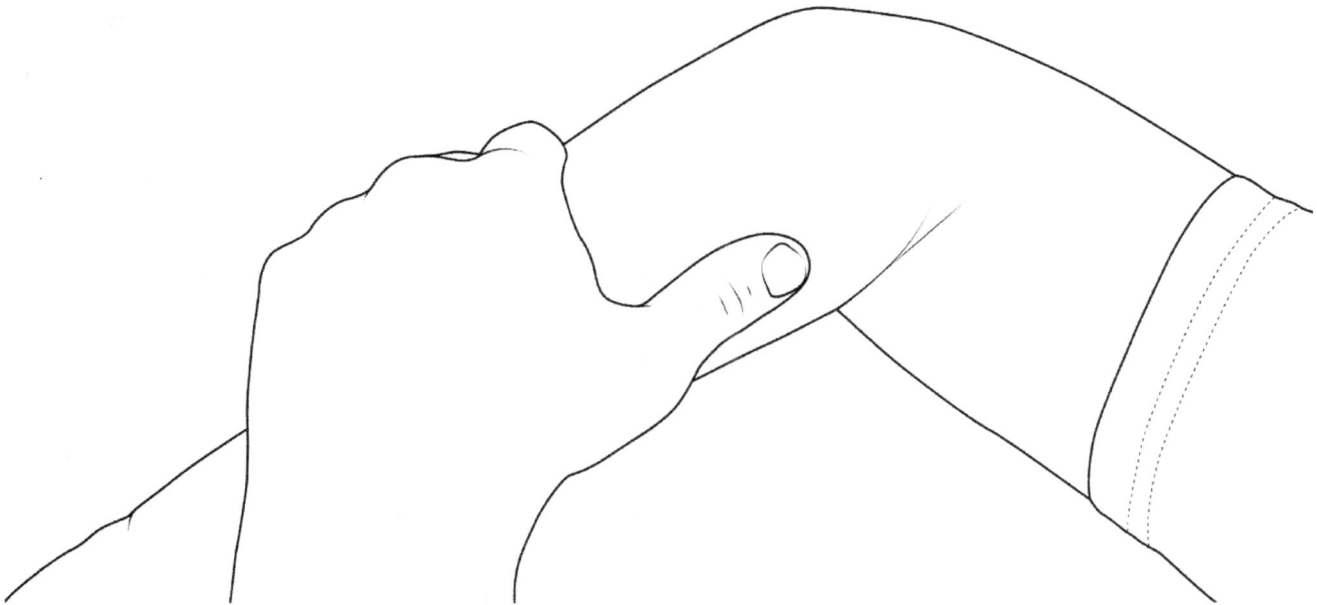

Finally, I loosen up my pectoral muscles beneath the clavicle bone. To do this, I place two fingers from my right hand at the centre of the left side of my upper chest, just under the clavicle.

Applying a little pressure, I make anticlockwise circles with my fingers, moving the circles out towards the armpit, an inch at a time.

After thirty seconds on one side, I switch sides and use two fingers of my left hand to massage my right side.

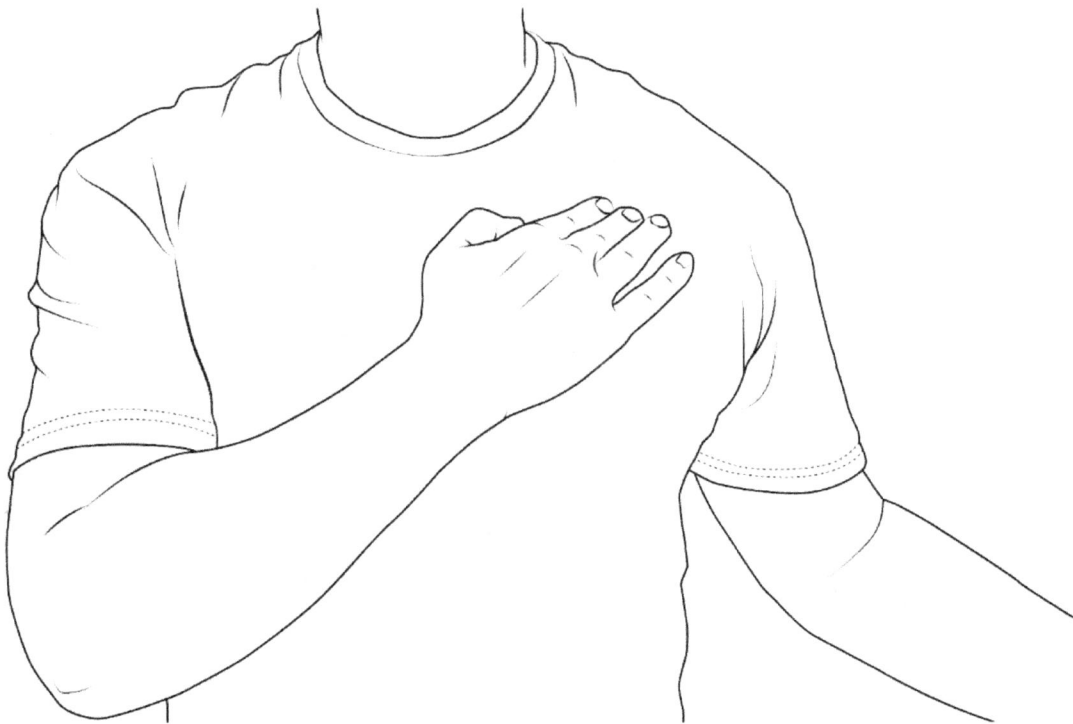

With the muscles primed for playing, let's talk about seated posture.

It's important to position the guitar to allow it to sit comfortably and ergonomically. I want my hands to *play* the guitar, not hold it up.

The first thing I do to optimise my posture is to sit straight in a chair that allows my feet to rest flat on the floor with my knees bent at ninety degrees. I don't even want my calf muscles to get tense.

I rest my guitar in what many call the "classical position" on my left (non-dominant side) leg and use a footstool under that foot. As formal as it sounds, this positioning allows my guitar to sit perfectly and be ready for playing – even without a strap or before I rest my forearm on the guitar's body.

My strap length is adjusted to have very little slack in the seated position. I can stand up and have the guitar in a similar position, which removes the issue of not being able to play standing up, things I have practiced sitting down. It doesn't make me look as cool as Slash, but it provides consistency.

Resting the guitar on your dominant leg is fine too, if you can sustain hours of playing in that position. After years of using that approach, I found myself twisting my body and not keeping my shoulders level when I wasn't playing the guitar.

If you have felt a bit twisted in the "rock position" or that your guitar is not fully supported, try the classical position and see how it feels.

Now that you're set up and loosened up, let's move into the warmup routines.

Routine One: Picking Hand Focus

Looking at the examples ahead, you'll undoubtedly notice all the X markings in the tablature. This routine focuses solely on the picking hand for various alternate-, sweep-, and economy-picked warmups.

For the duration of this routine, choke all the strings by lightly barring the fingers of your fretting hand. Doing so will allow complete focus on executing all the pick strokes accurately.

Try four repeats of each drill as a starting point. In future practice sessions, each repetition can be played faster than before. If you need more time on any exercise, repeat as many times as necessary.

The first example is a string-crossing drill for alternate picking. Each string begins on a downstroke.

Example 1a:

Example 1b drops a note from the beginning of the drill, forcing the pick to land on new strings with upstrokes.

Example 1b:

Addressing outside picking, where the pick travels the longest distance between strings, Example 1c increases the gaps between strings throughout bar one, decreasing them again in bar two.

Accuracy is paramount for this drill, so don't begin too fast.

Example 1c:

Let's apply progressive string skipping distances using inside picking – the most direct route for each string change.

Example 1d:

Alternate picking odd numbers of notes per string will see the pick switch between hitting new strings on downstrokes and upstrokes. Be sure to repeat this drill seamlessly, with consistent timing in either direction.

Example 1e:

We can exaggerate the string changing of the previous drill by reintroducing string skips.

Example 1f:

The next drill is excellent for focused rest strokes and direction changes for sweep picking.

Each stroke should see the pick land directly on the following string, rather than having separate successive downstrokes and upstrokes. You'll see this in action in the video for this routine.

Example 1g:

Let's begin with the higher strings this time. Each bar starts with an upward (descending) sweep.

Example 1h:

Now that you've warmed up sweeping string changes, let's apply that to scalar picking.

Example 1i uses downstroke sweeping for ascending string changes and upward sweeping for descending string changes.

This is a perfect way to internalise the mechanics of economy picking before fretting scales with the other hand.

Example 1i:

Lastly, let's do six-string sweeps in both directions, remembering to land the pick on each string straight out of the previous string.

Example 1j:

To ease the fretting hand into playing for the day, Routine Two comprises chord work, while Routine Three addresses linear fretting drills.

Routine Two: Chordal Warmup

This routine is designed to ease your fingers into playing by using some diatonic and atonal chord shapes.

First up, we'll get the four fingers of the fretting hand onto the fretboard in a diagonal row, with the index finger on the highest string of each group, down to the pinkie finger on the lowest string.

Strum each shape once before moving a fret higher and changing string groups after four strums. The same frets are used for each string group without regard for playing in a key.

For the curious, moving the shape along the lower string group (bars one and seven) spells out a series of augmented triads. The same shape on the middle strings (bars two and six) outlines augmented major 7 chords. On the top string group (bars three and five), we get unaltered major 7 chords.

Example 2a:

Now let's isolate pairs of fingers using dyads at two angles.

Throughout this drill, each finger (1-2-3-4) is assigned to the same fret (5-6-7-8) of each relevant string.

Example 2b:

Next, we'll transition through four angular shapes per bar. The shape on beat one of each bar is fretted using the index finger on the lowest note, down to the pinkie, then we move two fingers on each successive beat. In subsequent bars, the pattern repeats on the next string group.

When you've mastered these transitions, you can exaggerate the exercise by moving to lower frets.

Fans of John Petrucci's *Rock Discipline* video course might also be accustomed to putting empty frets between fingers for some wild stretches (e.g., frets 4-6-7-8, 5-6-7-9 etc), but I suggest taking your time to really loosen up before taking things to the extreme.

Example 2c:

Getting diatonic, the next three examples use chord inversions to move around the neck for a more musical way of practicing.

In each of these drills, use the fingers to squeeze and release very short-sounding chords (*staccato*). This small finger flex adds an extra warmup element to the chord changes.

Use only enough pressure to sound the notes clearly to avoid a build-up of unnecessary tension.

Beginning this diatonic section, here's a C major triad played from open position up to a second inversion shape and downward.

Example 2d:

Here, we'll start from the first-inversion C major triad and use an octave of the open chord shape at the beginning of bars two and four. The latter shape will take some focus to fret accurately if this is your first time trying it.

Example 2e:

Using the same staccato approach, Example 2f is based on root position and first-inversion major 7 chords. Note where each finger needs to move from one shape to the next.

Bars three and four contain the same shapes as the first two bars, played a perfect 4th higher.

Example 2f:

For stretchier chord shapes, the following example is based on a moving "add11" shape that you might recognise from Joe Satriani's *Always With Me, Always With You*. The shape contains no 5th.

There's no key at play in this example. Instead, the idea is to play the chord shape up high where it's pretty manageable, then move down to where the stretches become progressively more challenging.

Instead of staccato playing like the last few examples, let each note in this example sustain while fretting.

Example 2g:

For the next stretchy chord change exercise, fingers one and four remain in the same spots. Fingers two and three are assigned to the same frets in each bar but swap strings between chords.

Example 2h:

As a chord-type transition exercise, Example 2i changes one chord tone each time by lowering it a semitone, moving from major 7 to dominant 7, and minor 7 to minor 7b5 chord types.

When the low E string note is flattened, we're ready to repeat the exercise a semitone lower (bar three) than where it began. You can move this exercise down like this as many times as you like.

Example 2i:

For the final chord stretch, we'll play two-octave power chords from the D string to the high E string, with whole-tone stretches between fingers one and two and fingers three and four.

Only move the shape down as many semitone steps as you can handle.

Example 2j:

The next section takes a single-note approach to warming up the fretting hand.

Routine Three: Linear Fretting Hand Warmup

Just as Routine One isolated the picking hand for extra attention, this routine isolates the fretting hand and uses no pick strokes (unless stated).

Most drills in this routine use hammer-ons to wake up the fingers, practice accurate fretting, and apply consistent finger pressure.

Ghost-note hammer-on indicators have been omitted to keep the notation clean, as you'll be articulating every note (for now) as a hammer-on in every direction.

Using the 1-2-3-4 diagonal finger shape from the previous routine, you'll sound out the notes in Example 3a by hammering each finger down, lifting the previous finger off, rather than stacking them on the fretboard.

Watch the accompanying video to see how I "roll" each finger into the next using my wrist. It's a pianistic approach, landing on the notes like the keys of a piano.

Try a fret wrap product to focus on the notes and avoid string noise. You could also loosely tie a sock around the lower frets or place your picking hand behind your fretting hand to silence the strings.

Example 3a:

We'll do the same thing in Example 3b, using the opposite diagonal shape.

Example 3b:

Using string pairs, the next drill uses fingers one and two on the lower string and fingers three and four on the higher string of each pair.

Aim for a flowing sound on each string and as you move across to the next.

Example 3c:

Using all four fingers on each string, Example 3d is one of the "24 Permutations" (the twenty-four possible combinations using 1-2-3-4 fingerings). Here, we're using fingers 1-3-2-4 and 4-2-3-1 in the 9th position.

Example 3d:

Example 3e uses 3-1-2-4 and 3-1-4-2 fingerings for some more excellent mental challenges.

Since you'll be going from higher to lower notes along the same string, lifting each finger off precisely before the next finger hammers down is crucial. Avoid doing any pull-offs for now, as we're still focusing on applying an even finger pressure.

Example 3e:

Okay, now we can do some pull-offs.

Example 3f uses fingers one to four with two position jumps along each string. A pull-off to the open string follows each hammer-on.

Example 3f:

The next drill uses slurs between the first and third fingers, then the second and fourth fingers, on each string.

You can continue this example down to the lowest string.

Example 3g:

The last legato drill uses a C Major scale fragment in two octaves. You can use the pick to initiate each string if you need to.

If scalar pull-offs like bars three and four are beyond your experience, try beginning each string with a pick stroke instead of a pinkie hammer-on. You can even use two pick strokes and one pull-off per string but keep the pick strokes soft, so as not to overpower the other notes.

Example 3h:

The Twenty-four Permutations of 1-2-3-4

For additional fretting practice and finger independence, here are the twenty-four ways we can arrange four fingers along a string (or even across them like examples 3a and 3b):

1-2-3-4	1-2-4-3	1-3-2-4	1-3-4-2	1-4-2-3	1-4-3-2
2-1-3-4	2-1-4-3	2-3-1-4	2-3-4-1	2-4-1-3	2-4-3-1
3-1-2-4	3-1-4-2	3-2-1-4	3-2-4-1	3-4-1-2	3-4-2-1
4-1-2-3	4-1-3-2	4-2-1-3	4-2-3-1	4-3-1-2	4-3-2-1

Routine Four: Chromatic Displacement Picking

Using both hands, the routine ahead will warm up your picking chops and tidy up your synchronisation (with even more synchronisation focus to come in Routine Eight).

I've called this routine "Chromatic Displacement" since the ideas are twists on the stock, standard four-finger chromatic drills.

The first three drills use the 1-2-3-4 fingering, but the notes are spread across the strings in less conventional ways.

Example 4a places three of the notes on one string, and the last note on the following string. Every other ascending iteration does the same. From bar three, beat 3, where the drill descends, the fourth note in each row is displaced to a lower string.

Example 4a:

Next, we'll evenly split the four fingers between string pairs, beginning each new set on the same string as the previous set finished.

Example 4b:

Continuing the displacement idea one more step, Example 4c retains only one note on the first string of each four-note iteration.

Example 4c:

Example 4d provides a rhythmic challenge comprised of ten-note chromatic phrases played as 1/8th note triplets.

The string changes fall in unusual places within the bar, so keeping it together and being mindful of the beat is a fun quest.

Following this drill, Example 4e provides its descending counterpart.

Example 4d:

Example 4e:

The next drill is a good speed warmup, as the fretting pattern is less daunting than others.

A descending version of the pattern appears in bar four, moving down into 6th position and connecting back to 5th position for the repeats.

Try this drill a little faster on each repeat.

Example 4f:

Crossing strings with only one picked note per string is one of the hardest things to do fast on a guitar. Constantly switching between picking inside the strings and around them, Example 4g uses our well-worn diagonal four-string patterns across string groups.

The last drill puts the focus on fingers three and four.

Example 4j:

In the next section, we'll use alternate picking for a scale-based routine.

Routine Five: Major and Minor Scales

Scales should be a mainstay of every developing guitarist's practice regimen, so this routine will be good developmental material for those playing scales for the first time and a more musical way to warm up for the advancing player.

For good fretboard coverage and versatility, I recommend learning scales from what I called "4-2-1 perspectives" when I was starting out: scales that begin with the fourth finger, second finger, and first finger.

Here's what I mean, demonstrated using a C Major scale. Each line of Example 5a works a different pattern to outline the same two-octave scale.

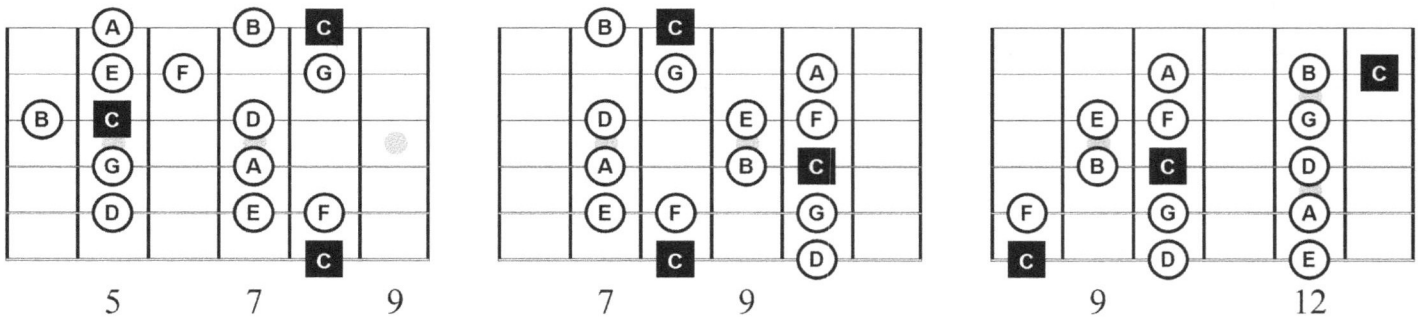

Example 5a:

Doing the same for the C Minor scale looks like this.

Example 5b:

```
      9                                10                            11                            12
T|----------------------------------|----------------------------|------------------------------|----------------------|
A|----------------------------------|--------------9—11—13—11----|--9---------------------------|----------------------|
B|--------------------------8—10----|----8—10—12-----------------|-----12—10—8------------------|--10—8----------------|
 |--------------8—10—11-------------|--12------------------------|-----------12—10—8------------|-----------11—10—8----|
 |--8—10—11-------------------------|----------------------------|----------------------11------|--11------------------|
```

Sequences (melodic units that move through a scale) also make great warmup exercises.

Here is the C Major scale played as a "3rds sequence" using the second pattern from Example 5a. The simple way to think of this sequence is to skip every second note, then return to it.

Playing this abbreviated scale version is a great way to internalise the sequences and work on outside picking (ascending) and inside picking (descending).

Example 5c:

```
      C                           2                              3                              4
     ∏  V  ∏  V  ∏  V  ∏  V
T|-------------------------------|-----------------7-----9------|--7---------------------------|------------------------|
A|-------------------7-----------|--9—7—10—9---------10---------|----9—10—7—9------7-----------|--10—7—8--------7-------|
B|--------7-----8—7—10—8---------|--10-------------------------|--------------10------8-------|----------10----8—10—7--|
 |--8----10---------------------|------------------------------|------------------------------|------------------------|
```

A little trickier, the following sequence is known as "ascending threes," where three ascending notes are played from each scale degree.

Example 5d:

"Descending threes" is the opposite sequence, moving down three notes at a time from each descending degree of the scale.

Example 5e:

Practicing scales around the Circle of Fourths is a neat way to move patterns around different keys and to learn the fretboard.

The Circle of Fourths (same as the Circle of Fifths but in the opposite direction) is a visual representation of major and minor keys and the sharps and flats contained within each. The circle illustrates the keys moving from one to the next in perfect 5ths (C Major, G Major, D Major etc) in the clockwise direction and perfect 4ths (C Major, F Major, Bb Major, etc) in the anti-clockwise direction.

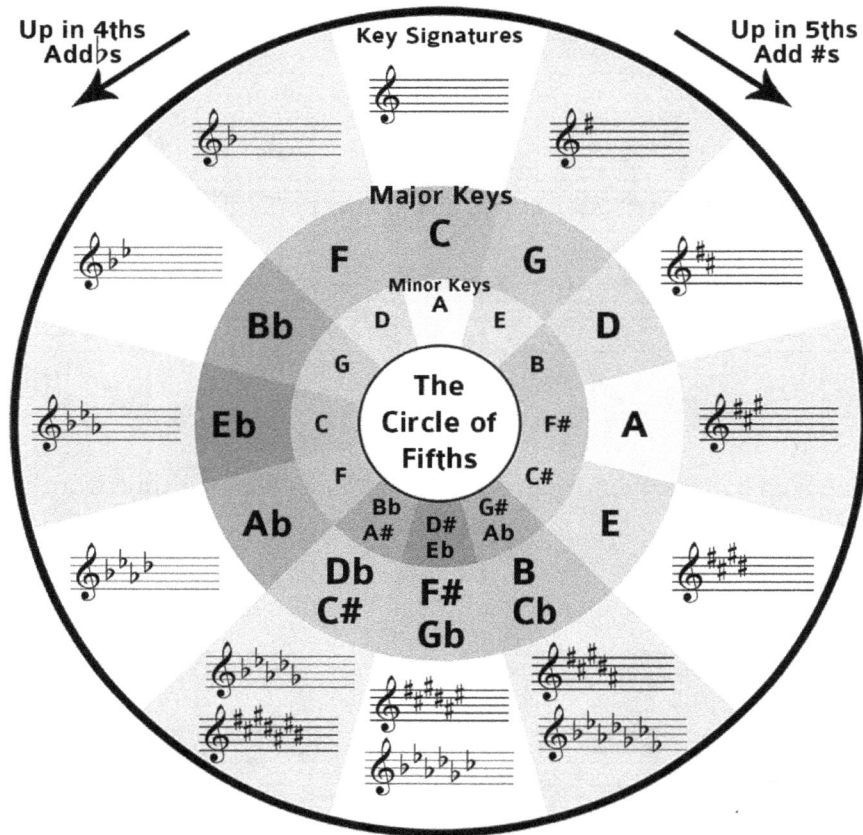

In the next drill, we'll play a one-octave C Major scale beginning on the A string, then move it around the circle in various octaves and positions.

Because of the major 3rd interval between the G and B strings on a standard-tuned guitar, the scale shapes will vary when moving the root note from the A string to the D and G strings.

Example 5f:

Diatonic 4th intervals work well for sequences and provide plenty of opportunities to warm the fingers up with rolling fingerings.

As you can see in examples 5g and 5h, playing in 4ths almost always means using the same finger between strings. Unlike barre chords, where we want the notes to ring together, these sequences require you to "roll" your finger from one string to the next.

39

Example 5g:

When you can play the 4ths sequence in both directions, combine Example 5g with the previous drill.

Example 5h:

Here's the C Minor scale played in 4ths too.

Example 5i:

To complete our scale warmup routine, here's a busier picking sequence in the key of C Minor. It uses the three-note-per-string shape shown in the last four bars of Example 5b.

This sequence goes up and down the scale with various turnaround points.

While the pick strokes indicated reflect alternate picking, the run is also a great candidate for economy picking.

Example 5j:

Next up, we'll look at an arpeggio-based warmup routine.

Routine Six: Arpeggios

Arpeggios are an essential unit of musical language and make great warmups too.

In this routine, we'll work through triads, 7th arpeggios, and Circle of Fourths exercises.

Here's a transition exercise, beginning with a C major triad played in two separate octaves (bars one and two).

With each chord change, one note from the previous triad is lowered. First, we lower the 3rd to get a C minor triad, then the 5th to get a C diminished triad.

Finally, by lowering the root, we end up back at a major triad but a semitone lower than where we began. You can use this exercise to trickle down the fretboard for as many steps as possible.

Example 6a:

With a repeated *down-down-up* picking pattern, Example 6b moves a different major triad shape through the Circle of Fourths.

Example 6b:

Example 6c:

Just as we played scales beginning with the fourth, second, and first fingers, we can do so with arpeggios. Let's create drills out of C major and C minor triads.

Example 6d:

Expanding to 7th arpeggios, the next transition exercise moves through C major 7th, dominant 7th, minor 7th, and half-diminished arpeggios, returning to a major 7th arpeggio from a B root note.

Like Example 6a, this drill can be moved through as many positions as you like.

Example 6e:

In the next drill, we'll move the major 7th shape in perfect 4ths again.

Example 6f:

The final drill for this routine is long, combining the ascending tonic triad and descending major scale of each key in the Circle of Fourths.

Example 6g:

Hopefully, this routine will contribute to your musical growth and your mechanical upkeep. See what other concepts you can practice using the Circle of Fourths.

In the next section, we'll look at a fingerpicking warmup routine.

Routine Seven: Fingerpicking

If you'd like to get the picking hand digits working, here's the routine to do it.

The drills in this section all use fingerpicking technique, including some hybrid picking (pick and fingers), with open and barre chord shapes.

In the notation ahead, you'll see the picking hand strokes indicated with **p** (*pulgar,* thumb), **i** (*indice,* first finger), **m** (*medio,* second finger), and **a** (*anular,* third finger).

In the first drill, fret the A minor and D minor open chords as indicated and hold them down for two bars each.

With your picking hand, pluck the open string root notes with the thumb. Pluck the notes on the adjacent string pair with the first and second fingers, then use the second and third fingers for the next string pair.

Example 7a:

This time, the root note will be plucked by the thumb on beats 1 and 3 throughout, using E major and A minor open chords.

Example 7b:

Now it's time to try some arpeggiation using an open C major chord.

In Example 7c, the thumb is assigned to the A and D strings. The first, second, and third fingers take care of the G, B, and E strings when each is called upon.

Example 7c:

Rather than always plucking in the order of p-i-m-a, we can apply permutations to fingerpicking patterns. In this exercise, each bar uses a slightly different picking pattern, with the fingers still assigned to their respective strings.

Example 7d:

48

Let's practice leading with the third finger using a cascading picking pattern this time.

Example 7e:

Next, we'll skip some strings so that our fingers aren't always picking adjacent strings.

This drill moves through an open E minor chord and barred G major, A minor, and B7 chords.

Example 7f:

Taking a hint from *Road Trippin'* by the Red Hot Chili Peppers, this drill adds 1/16th notes to the rhythm and uses root + 5th C major, D major, and E minor chords beginning on the A string.

Take your time getting the rhythm and the thumb/finger interplay right.

Example 7g:

The last three drills in this routine focus on hybrid picking, sometimes stylistically referred to as *chicken pickin'*.

The idea is to grip the pick with the thumb and first finger, assign picking duties to the second and third fingers, and pick/pluck with a combination of both.

Example 7h would be at home in a country or southern rock track, so don't be afraid to try it with some overdrive.

Example 7h:

Creating a *forward roll* with the pick, middle, and third fingers, Example 7i uses an A minor barre chord for training purposes.

You can let the chord ring out when developing the picking for this drill.

Example 7i:

For the last example, we'll use hybrid picking in more of a lead guitar drill. We want single notes only with no bleed into the other notes.

This drill will also sound great with overdrive, especially if you like fusion players like Brett Garsed.

Example 7j:

If this routine has been your first foray into fingerpicking, give yourself time to coordinate the fingers of your picking hand.

Routine Eight: Synchronisation

Getting the hands to work together is such an important subject that I wrote a book called *137 Guitar Speed & Coordination Exercises* on the topic.

In this routine, we'll address synchronisation in a tidy format that you can do quickly, anytime you need.

One of the best ways I've found to help the hands lock in together is to challenge conventional playing habits by twisting them in practice drills.

Here's a simple idea to get started.

Example 8a uses frets 5-8 on the G string in a chromatic row. Bar one contains four of each note, but the four C notes on the 5th fret are split between one note at the beginning and three at the end of the bar.

Many people find the note placements a challenge to keep locked in with the pick, since they occur on the second 1/16th note of each beat instead of with the downstrokes at the beginning of each beat.

See how fast you can get this without losing the beat.

Example 8a:

Now let's try one with some position jumps and slides without trying to "reset" where the notes change, or which pick strokes they correspond to.

Example 8b:

Finger independence is another crucial aspect of coordination.

Each beat of this drill focuses on a different finger pair. Each drill cycle takes three beats, then repeats on the same string before a rest, then a string change.

Begin with the second finger on the 6th fret of each string.

Example 8c:

In another example of a 1-2-3-4 displacement exercise (see also Routine Four), the next drill displaces the third finger note in each group of four.

Combining ascending and descending versions of the drill without a break can be a challenge. The descent begins at bar two, beat 2. Notice how the picking changes from inside picking (moving the pick directly between the strings) to outside picking (working around the strings).

Example 8d:

Creating two versions of a pedal-tone lick, the next drill contains frequent pinkie finger usage and reverses the pick strokes associated with each finger.

For example, in bar one the 7th fret notes on the D string are always picked with a downstroke, the 10th fret with an upstroke, etc.

This is reversed in bars two and four as the lick is played as a permutation.

Example 8e:

Odd melodic note groups make for fabulous brain twisters for synchronisation.

Here, a five-note motif is played across steady 1/16th notes, forcing the picking into opposite strokes with each repeat.

Make sure you keep the rhythm going with this drill because it can be tempting to pause slightly each time the motif restarts with different pick strokes.

Example 8f:

```
∏ V ∏ V ∏ V ∏ V ∏ V ∏ V ∏ V ∏
-12—9—12—10—9—12—9—12—10—9—12—9—12—10—9       12—9—12—10—9—12—9—12—10—9—12—9—12—10—9
```

Here's another five-note idea. This time, we'll play across the bar lines and accent the first note of each five.

Example 8g:

```
∏ V ∏ V ∏ V ∏ V ∏ V ∏ V ∏ V ∏ V      ∏ V ∏ V ∏ V ∏ V ∏ V ∏ V ∏ V
8—12—8—10—12—8—12—8—10—12—8—12—8—10—12—8      12—8—10—12—8—12—8—10—12—8—12—8—10—12
```

Example 8h is a seven-note repetition phrase that can be moved to any string or scale.

It's a challenging phrase because it's essentially a three-note repetition pattern (frets 12, 10, 9) with an extra note thrown in every second time (10th fret) as a spanner in the works!

The drill is played across bars of 7/8 time. If you're inexperienced with playing in odd time signatures, try tapping an 1/8th note rhythm with your foot, picking two notes for every tap.

Example 8h:

The next coordination drill is about synchronising position jumps within a single-string scale.

Each position contains three notes, and the aim is to get the first finger (ascending) and fourth finger (descending) into position each time, without melodic or rhythmic disruption to the flow of the scale.

Example 8i:

To complete the routine, we'll do a true chromatic scale run that includes the notes usually omitted in 1-2-3-4 exercises.

Each string contains five notes until the high E string, using a pinkie slide to grab an extra note per string on the way up and the first finger to do so on the way down.

String changes do not uniformly occur on the same part of each beat, and each string will begin with the pick stroke opposite to the previous string.

You can also play this drill as an economy-picking run, using sweep-picking for most string changes.

Example 8j:

Routine Nine: Fretting Hand Stretches

I said in the beginning that I don't believe warmups should be overly strenuous. Now that you've completed plenty of routines from the book, you can use any earlier material to prepare for a little more stretch for your fingers in this routine.

A gentle way to add stretching work to your practice routines is with minor 3rd intervals between fingers one and three, then two and four. By starting on the upper frets, you can ease into stretching, moving to lower frets if you want more of a challenge.

In the first drill, bar one is fretted using the first and third fingers. Bar two uses fingers two and four.

Example 9a:

Next, we'll try a whole tone stretch between neighbouring fingers. Play this drill using finger pairs one and two, two and three, three and four. Take care to avoid strain, and feel free to begin even higher on the neck, changing positions as indicated to increase the stretch each time.

Example 9b:

To use four fingers on a string with whole tone stretches between each, it's important to learn how to roll the notes using your wrist. Watch the accompanying video to see how I do this without relying on the fingers alone to reach each fret.

Example 9c:

Building on Example 9a, we can mix minor 3rd finger pairs in a more sequenced way across the strings.

Example 9d:

Here's the same approach with whole tone spaces between pairs of fingers (one and two, three and four).

Example 9e:

Applying sweep picking to a suspended 2nd arpeggio, this drill begins up high and can be lowered one fret each time for a progressively increased stretch.

Descend only as far as you're comfortable with.

Example 9f:

Calling upon the C Whole-Half Diminished scale (a synthetic scale comprised of alternating whole tones and semitones), Example 9g has a six-fret span from the first finger to the fourth, with the second and third fingers just a semitone apart in the middle.

Example 9g:

Like Example 9c, the next drill consists of a three whole-tone stretch but separates the notes into a wide stretch between fingers one and four with a whole-tone stretch one string higher with the other fingers.

The pattern goes up and down in each string pair before descending in octaves. The lower the octave, the more exaggerated the stretch.

Example 9h:

To end the routine, Example 9i sequences a whole-tone scale (another synthetic scale consisting of whole-tone steps only).

To stay within the scale, there's a two-fret jump between the G and B strings instead of the single-fret jump to the other strings.

Example 9i:

In the last routine, we'll get a bit wacky and nonsensical for fun!

Routine Ten: Wacky Drills

To conclude the book, here's a routine comprising bigger challenges and unorthodox drills.

Make sure you're well-warmed up from, say, routines one and two, before attempting this set.

Example 10a begins the routine with diagonal string changes sectioned into finger pairs.

The fingering will make sense after just a couple of repeats, but the picking will remain a nice string-changing challenge as it involves a lot of cross-picking.

Example 10a:

The next drill uses power chord shapes between the first and third fingers, then the second and fourth fingers.

Outside picking is used on the way up, switching to inside picking on the way down.

For an added challenge, an 1/8th note triplet rhythm is used, which can feel at odds with the motif, which is based on two-note segments.

Example 10b:

The best way I can describe what's happening in the following angular picking drill is that it's like painting a rectangle from one corner to the diagonally opposite corner.

At the heart of the drill is a series of diagonal one-note-per-string rows, with fewer notes in the "corners" at the beginning and end of the drill.

Example 10c:

For some string-skipping with 1-2-3-4 fingering exercises, Example 10d zig-zags between strings, changing to new strings at peculiar points in each bar.

Steady rhythm is crucial, so begin slow enough to play evenly across all the string changes.

Example 10d:

The next two drills are three-note versions of the previous drill.

Firstly, it's played from the 5th fret using the first three fingers.

To up the challenge, the version afterward is played using fingers two, three, and four only. When playing this, let your first finger hover over the strings, but not too far away from the fretboard.

Example 10e:

Example 10f:

Included as an exaggeration exercise for outside picking, this drill begins with alternate picking between the adjacent D and G strings before skipping not one but two strings as it moves to the A and B strings.

The speed at which you can play the latter string change will determine your speed for the whole drill.

Example 10g:

Lastly, we'll mix a diagonal finger pair with 4-3-2-1 and 1-2-3-4 exercises.

For speed purposes, I use my first and second fingers, with position jumps for the angular sections that begin each bar.

Example 10h:

Building a Custom Warmup Routine

After you've gone through all the material in the ten curated routines, you might like to customise your warmups based on your daily practice goals.

If your aim for today is to practice alternate picking, you can assemble a selection of suitable warmups from the ninety-two examples in this book.

Here's a sample routine for a customised alternate picking warmup.

Custom Alternate Picking Warmup No. 1:

Drill	Targeted Area	Frequency
Example 1a	Picking hand isolation	Four repeats
Example 1e	Picking hand isolation	Four repeats
Example 3d	Fretting hand isolation	Four repeats
Example 4a	Chromatic displacement	Four repeats
Example 4d	Chromatic displacement	Four repeats
Example 5a	Major scale coverage	Four repeats
Example 5c	Scale sequencing – 3rds	Four repeats
Example 5g	Scale sequencing – 4ths	Four repeats

A more advanced alternate picking warmup might look like this:

Custom Alternate Picking Warmup No. 2:

Drill	Targeted Area	Frequency
Example 3a	Fretting hand isolation	Four repeats
Example 4g	Cross picking	Four repeats
Example 4i	Finger independence	Four repeats
Example 5d	Ascending threes sequence	Four repeats
Example 5e	Descending threes sequence	Four repeats
Example 5j	Minor scale sequence	Four repeats
Example 8h	Synchronisation	Four repeats
Example 8j	Synchronisation	Four repeats
Example 10a	Unorthodox picking patterns	Four repeats

You might compile a list of directional picking warmups for sweep- and economy-picking. Here's one you can try that combines chromatic and diatonic drills.

Custom Sweep/Economy Picking Warmup:

Drill	Targeted Area	Frequency
Example 1g	Isolated sweep picking	Four repeats
Example 1h	Isolated sweep picking	Four repeats
Example 1i	Isolated sweep picking	Four repeats
Example 2h	Chordal warmup with sweep picking	Four repeats
Example 2j	Chordal warmup with sweep picking	Four repeats
Example 4h	Chromatic displacement sweeping	Four repeats
Example 5b	Minor sales with economy picking	Four repeats
Example 6b	Sweep-picked triads in 4ths	Four repeats
Example 8j	5-note-per-string chromatics with economy picking	Four repeats

Almost all the material in this book can be retooled for different applications or new challenges for your technique and brain.

Here are some suggestions for reworking drills in the book.

- Reverse pick strokes, e.g., begin exercises on the opposite pick strokes to those indicated

- Finger-pick all chordal warmups in Routine Two instead of using a pick

- Economy-pick all alternate picking examples that feature odd numbers of notes per string.

- Alternate-pick any sweep-picking material

- Increase stretches by selectively using whole-tone spacing between fingers on chromatic drills

- Move exercises one fret lower with each repeat

With enough imagination, you'll never need to spend hours looking for warmup drills again!

Conclusion

I hope you've enjoyed developing and implementing good warmup habits for your guitar practice.

It's worth reiterating that warming up should be a gradual process that avoids too much too soon.

Select material from this book as it pertains to your level of playing experience and allow it to elevate your chops progressively over the course of several warmups. As tempting as it might be to seek out the wildest examples to begin your practice, it's more sensible to work your way up.

When approaching more demanding material, ease in by preparing yourself with sufficient basic warmup examples, like those found in the first few routines in the book.

The more respect you show your body and technique, the longer they'll serve you.

Enjoy your time in the practice room!

Chris Brooks

About the Author

Chris Brooks has set new standards for the calibre of guitar technique books. With a flair for what makes things tick, his depth of understanding of guitar mechanics has helped tens of thousands of readers worldwide.

Playing guitar since September 1987, Chris took early inspiration from Brett Garsed, Kee Marcello, Vinnie Moore, and Yngwie Malmsteen, practicing feverishly through his teens.

Educated at the Australian Institute of Music under the tutelage of Dieter Kleeman, Ike Isaacs, and Carl Orr, Chris developed a passion for guitar education that resulted in managing a music school with close to a thousand private students per week in Sydney's western suburbs.

Focusing on online education and product development in the last decade, Chris has written over a dozen best-selling guitar books, created scores of video products, and released two acclaimed instrumental rock albums.

You can learn more at **www.chrisbrooks.com**

Other titles by Chris Brooks

Neoclassical Speed Strategies for Guitar

Sweep Picking Speed Strategies for Guitar

Advanced Arpeggio Soloing for Guitar

7-string Sweep Picking Speed Strategies for Guitar

Legato Guitar Technique Mastery

100 Arpeggio Licks for Shred Guitar

The Complete Guitar Technique Speed Strategies Collection

Alternate Picking Guitar Technique

Economy Picking Guitar Technique

Rock Guitar Tapping Technique

Chris Brooks' 3-in-1 Picking & Tapping Guitar Technique Collection

137 Guitar Speed & Coordination Exercises

Pentatonic Speed Strategies for Guitar

1980s Rock Rhythm Guitar Mastery

13 Week Guitar Technique Bootcamp

https://www.fundamental-changes.com/product-tag/chris-brooks/